Enhancing a New Start

Enhancing a New Start

TAMEAKEI FLOWERS

authorHOUSE®

AuthorHouse™
1663 Liberty Drive
Bloomington, IN 47403
www.authorhouse.com
Phone: 1 (800) 839-8640

Published by AuthorHouse 10/09/2015

ISBN: 978-1-5049-5583-6 (sc)
ISBN: 978-1-5049-5582-9 (e)

Hiding within

A time in our life we hide behind these walls of guilt and shame

People we thought we can trust,

Later on we found out we can't

It's the strongest Christian whose spreading rumors about another Christian who not so strong who needed a friend to talk to

She confided in a stronger Christian for comforting not knowing her information was leaving the individual she confiding in

It ended up a down fall because now she wondering how can I face another Christian about my problem and not end up in the same situation

because now she thinking when you confiding in someone she wondering if her information still with the person or it's leaving

A believer you didn't expect to do something like that ended up to be your worst enemy

Now you wondering why this person could do something like this especially a believer you look up to

You see you shouldn't look at it as a downfall but as a growth with God spiritually as well as naturally because instead of putting your trust in human you need to start putting your trust in God. God will never leave you but people comes and go.

Always know not every person who goes to church are Christian. The devil goes to church as well. Now you know that God is your friend and know that whatever you going through always know you can come to him. Let this be a growth to you and not be a let down in your life but a closer walk with God and forgive this person because You want someone to forgive you even God. A lesson to be learn

Burning with Lust in the mind

Now let me tell you all this is in the mind

You went to two parents about their son's

They both son's started off with wanting sex getting me to play the mind game

You didn't fall for it

So one of the guy ended up getting serious and he was praying for a women

The other guy started hating you for no reason

You started going to church and the guy you expected to be the one praying to be with you

Ended up being the guy you in church thinking having sexual sin with and he's laughing about it

The other guy you didn't expect when he comes to church you don't

But it started off that way

You realize that both of them are friends and it shows you that sin is also in the church and you shouldn't go to church all kind of how. You should put your focus on the word and what God is telling you through his mouth piece. Let this be a lesson learn that you allow God to send you someone and know that and know every guy that goes to church is saved and the one for you either. Put your focus and trust in God and see the outcome. Watch him move in your life

Another incident with burning with lust in the mind

It all started when you got older and given your life to God

The comes with obstacles to block you from getting to know God

Remind you it's a mind game

you trying to do what's right and all of a sudden the enemy pops up

Getting you to believe that this actually happen

Now let me tell you it's nothing but family member wanting sex

And not every family member are like that we have good not so good family member, but all your family member having odds against you for what no reason

okay here goes

parents having sex around you, cousins forcing themselves on you girl and boy cousin threaten you as well, being watch

while naked, while being naked a family member doing whatever to wake you so you can see him or naked

So that trigger a button because now you started believing what the devil has played in your mind and started a warfare with those people in real life

And that build up tension between yawl now you thinking revenge on this matter

You see how the devil played with your mind with lust building up anger in you

So there can be tension between the family and nothing else

You gotta realize that the enemy is playing you like a deck of cards

like for instance a guy and you suppose to be dating

One moment he with you and then the next he wanting somebody else, moving from women to women and after he had all these women and he catch something now he wants you hugging you kissing you, wanting you

Where was him when you needed him

He was thinking about pleasing his flesh not having the person he supposed to be with on his mind

I came to a conclusion that all guys are not like that if he really truly wants to be with you then he wouldn't allow these other women trigger him into sex or allowing this women

clothes draw him to you. We all make mistakes but every time you make one, saying you go do what's right and go right back out there making the mistake over and over again. Actually you didn't mean it because for one if you did your mind will be on her and doing what's right by here trying to make it work. But you don't do it that way the only thing you have in mind is you pleasing your flesh not thinking about who you're harming and hurting

These incident happen in real life don't take it for granted take it in and applied to your life daily. You will never know the time and place this might happen to you if it already happen be consider when someone is trying to help be thankful amen

Secrecy

When you think you getting away with stuff

You not

People have a tendency of doing stuff and thinking they getting away with it

when the truth is God is watching and you think people not seeing you actually they is what you do in the dark will come to the light

And when it does your business done out and you worrying about what go said about you for one you shouldn't did what you did

and two you must be want it out

so obviously you must be fond about your information being spread around the world if not you wouldn't expose yourself

Let's talk about this incident and after we have two more

okay here goes

You walking minding your own business this guy come up to you and wanting your number you turn him down Remind you

You doing what's right by God

one incident these guys know that you're weak in an area so he use that against you

So you minding your business again and the same guy stop asking you for your number

Not mentioning anything about his girlfriend whether he have one or not

If he did he wouldn't tell you but let's was honest with you and tell you he had someone that should give you signal to walk away he's off limit it also saying I really like you and if you can wait until I break it off then we can be together another option is I might be off limit if you down with this then we can mess around. Now by him telling you about her you have a choice walk away or sin

Now without him telling you that's a whole different story if he truly cared you he would be honest and also not approach you and two he wouldn't go out an look for another girl if he truly loved the one he with. Anyway that's a sin looking at another man wife or messing with another person that's not yours it's sin you committing adulterous Either way you dead wrong because the bible said no sex without marriage and no fornication outside of your marriage

Another incident was when you and a group of people was headed to work

And this guy he does things to get your scared up

In his mind you a target but in yours you thinking you scared and this guy doesn't have any chance to get with you

This girl on the van and this guy was messing around he does things to her on the van to make her do what he said

The same guy approach you the van stop there was nobody on the van but yawl he call you back you went he unbuckled his pants and commanded you to do the same you did Thank God somebody was watching because if that person wasn't watching no telling what would of happen. Every time you to that location with guys they after you trying to get with you so they can get between your pants. Even though they with someone

The three incident was when you laid with the father of your child. To you, you thinking this is the one not knowing this is a one night stand. You no these guys have a way to convincing you and you fall for it. That showing him you let anybody take advantage of you. Moving along by him making that move on you you decided to lay with this dude by him asking you you agree yawl laid with each other you conceived a child the two of you. You felt the baby being birth inside of you. You called him and let him know that you felt funny. He didn't cared he went his way. So you started feeling like throwing up but I didn't. I couldn't lay on my stomach and sometimes on my right side because that's my babies side. I found out that you was pregnant when you went to the clinic. During your pregnancy you was upset because in your mind you thinking if you going to be a good mom or if you have what it takes to be a parent, also you will messed

up by raising or your child will be taken. You had all these thoughts playing around in your head. Making you doubt yourself. You didn't even tell the father of your child because you didn't trust him or any men with your daughter without you being around or the police. Because there are rapers out their and you don't know what's running through any man or any body mind. So you careful who your child goes to. While your child inside you yawl had this connection. You knew in your heart that she wanted you to know that she was a girl. Even though others was telling you what think she is but you didn't accept what they had to said. You went by what you and your daughter said she was. The baby daddy call you with nothing but foolishness. He doesn't come and see his child that he help created. He don't even buy or they both doesn't know how each other look. The only people she know is the mother side not the father.

You been through so much financially, raising her up as well because even though you was helped out a family member or a friend it's not like your own until you have one. Giving birth to you wasn't so bad it was the pushing and the pain when it's time for you to push. Other than that you had an learning experience but don't you go out and have sex without marry again because you might not be lucky the next time and sometimes a condom doesn't. If you love you then don't take that risk of harming yourself. Take it from somebody who been their. Knowing your business have left into the world by people who knew and been capable of spreading, having their friends calls you names, looking at you in a different way

The bible speaks that you should not fight against flesh and blood, but why as Christian we can't see each other as brother and sister in Christ

which we

We might not be blood related but in Christ Jesus we related because if you have Christ in your life then we are brother and sister in Christ Jesus We should be lifting one another up instead of tearing each other down. Don't fight against flesh and blood but against dark rulers of high places that's trying to stop the purpose of God to move in your life. Instead we fighting one another like trying to stop a growth in a person by you speaking the opposite of what God says going to happen

You spoke a new life by this person you call friend was going to loose his or her virginity. This friend confiding in you and you wasn't being a friend because if you were you wouldn't lead this friend into the wrong path. Now this friend heartbroken because he or she trusted you not expecting a church person would do something like this.

Here it goes again where a church member gets involve by leading this person down the wrong path of sin. Even though this person had a mind of his own. The point is they both was wrong because if this person was a friend she wouldn't lead that person down the path of sin and if that person had a mind he or she would have say no. You see the church member should have stay in their place regardless if they knew the person who the person they consider a friend came and told them about. They should have put a stop to it in the beginning. You not knowing if this person had a girl friend

or not you trusted your friend with what she was telling you. Guys consider it a guy friend or girl as friends. You would want to know especially if they consider you a friend. They wouldn't anything bad to happen too happen to you because they cared and love you. Also with this person girlfriend coming to your house. Now he's acting like he doesn't know you calling you names, cussing you out. The honest truth is deep inside you learned your lesson because if these guys truly loved you. He wouldn't pursue you. He would have left you alone but he didn't. You ended up hurt in the process of it but thank God it was nothing else because you could have been dead or laying in the hospital bill. You gotta be careful who you open your heart open to. It might not be a heartbroken the time let this be a lesson learned okay

The same so call friend knew your weakness and wanted to used your weakness against you. Like for instance the money this person knew you was kind person who has giving heart. So this person knew that and try to take advantage of it even though it was success by you giving this money on the side. This person came to you about a situation matter fact a bill problem wanting a certain amount you went to the somebody else about the matter they denied you doing it because they been through that situation and the person knew they didn't needed the money, so you ended up keeping the money. But the person try it again and kept on trying now they not.

We allow obstacles to come to tear us apart instead of defeating the purpose of the enemy

We keep our mouth shut and not say a thing

you allow the devil to have access our data

We suppose to be Christian not allowing the enemy to rap us of our glory by us keeping our mouth close

We need to get out of no talking phase and get into a talking state of mind

And allow the enemy to know where his place at in line not the front

But to the back of the line matter fact not even in the line because he's not capable of handling what God has in stored for his people

Matter fact he's the opposite of God he's the enemy

Instead of dwelling on the past how about letting it go and focus on the now

By taking one step at a time and not concentrate on the things that's not taking you no where

Take the past as a growth walk with God because by you dwelling on that you just hinder yourself from prospering in the future and your walk with God spiritually as well naturally. Use your past as learning and a helping mode. You will be able to learn from your mistakes and help others overcome their mistakes you witnessing to someone that lay upon your heart to do

Don't allow your past build up tense in your life that you put up these walls stopping your future from flowing like for instance you in school to you and your eye sight you

not the smartest kid there. When it comes down to work you failing it depends on your teacher that's teaching you. But with the other students they making good grades in everything. You think! Your studying notes missing so you couldn't study, their was class clowns around so you couldn't get the education that you deserve. You started telling yourself negativity because you didn't see yourself a learning material So you started doubting God which we all do that God doesn't love you, look how he created you just all kinds of negativity stuff that you could think of to throw out their. You see! You gotta be careful what goes in and what comes out because what's in your heart the mouth speaks, so be careful because you don't want to get yourself into trouble by your mouth do you? I know I don't. Take this as a love note

We should tear down those walls to the gates of hell

And not allowing the enemy to have free course in our lives anymore

He has done worst to us by letting him be a guest in our bedroom

Give the devil his eviction notice evict him out of your apartment and open up to him every again

Now he's at a different apartment wanting to sign an agreement with the landlord Don't even give him that satisfaction of allowing him to live in your house with the glory of the lord dines at. You should put up a sign and seal the door post with power of the holy spirit.

Now the enemy moving up to college wanting to get acceptance in college

You shouldn't even give him the devil an application and not even let a foot in your office

Don't even give him acceptance to your school kick him out

By you taking back what the devil has stole from you

And stole being lack on your job because Satan doing what he suppose to be doing

do yours

Don't sit on your calling go out and make your calling known

We keep telling God we gonna change and do what's right by him

That just mouth we need action behind what we said

Every time we start off right and some thing doesn't go our way we either backslide or we throw in the tower and called it a quick just like baseball

We go a certain minute and when it gets tough we want to quick and not try again

Like when you up to hit the ball and the pitcher throwing the ball steadily throwing

Obviously you not hitting even though you doing your best

So you rounded up with three strikes and had to go out the game you didn't hit any ball to go too the base and it wasn't the pitcher fault. Just like you were determine to keep going you wasn't about to stop you wanted to hit a ball and make a home room that's what God wants to do in your life

win you so the devil won't

you gotta be careful who you serve because you can't serve two master you gotta hate one and love the other Don't let the enemy or nobody pressure you into do nothing you know not right and you feel comfortable doing

Complaining

As we burial our thoughts in sorrow and disgrace

we complaining to our God almighty about pitiful stuff that's not in our control to handle

As we keep dwelling in this place call the dark valley

Here we are blaming others for the pain we cause on ourselves

or

Allowing others to influence us to do wrong

But when the time comes we complaining about the mistakes

We never learned from

We keep doing the same thing over and over again

When will it ever stop?

Or

would it

How long must I suffer for you to see the hurt and pain

I have on the inside of me

Day in and day out

I crying to the Lord telling him I can't deal with this anymore

At times I want to throw in the tower because I can't face the stress of everyday life

I feel like people doesn't understand me and I can't see this problem that I'm facing

At times I go to bed and can't sleep because of what I'm going through

I tried putting it behind me and blocking it out of my mind

I just don't understand how to deal with this problem

At times I don't know if I going to live or die

All I want to do is live in harmony and not face the everyday life

We all go through it is up to us too determine in our mind and heart that we will not allow what keeping us get the best of us. We gotta get up everyday speaking greatness about ourselves we can't let our past, present, and future determine us we gotta determine our life. By planning our future we gotta let go of the past because we can't bring the past back. We gotta move on by accepting the past for what it is. If we keep dwelling on the past then there won't be no future for us. We gotta move forward and no this we can't change the past.

We got to understand that we gotta do better and not make that mistake every again and learned from the past

It take time we don't change over night. We gotta take one step at a time and no that people are praying and God is on your side helping you along the way. Don't feel discourage and left out because God is with you and he loves you. And Know that he always there to listen to talk and be a lover and friend

Life is a battle especially in our mind if we don't renewed daily then we have a battle on our hands

We should take our mind serious because if we don't take it from some one who been there we will loose our mind. You gotta read the bible daily and applied it to your life.

The enemy doesn't cared who he messed with you gotta be prayed up, fasting and speaking positive

because the enemy is lurking and he wants to know if you accept his behavior or put in his place

We gotta be determine to be in this race for real or not

Because there can't anybody being in this race and not finish

We gotta have a made up mind to go all the way and partial

It is up to you nobody can determine for you

Set Back

We set a lot of stuff back and not stick with what we set our mind to do

Is it because we have fear that's blocking us from stepping forward

We gotta overcome fear and step outside of something like college

If we know that we always start and not finish that is because we afraid of failing and not achieving

We gotta have a made up mind and know that no one is perfect

We all makes mistakes always know just because you not good at something that doesn't make you a failure nobody good at everything you gotta find your gift, something you good at pursue after it

Just know you not in this alone people are there willing to help

You just gotta put yourself known and trust God in all of this

Peace

God has given all of us a peace of mind

He doesn't want you lost in the wilderness

He want his sheep at ease and not frustrated

Just like in the army the commander order his cadets to be at ease

He doesn't want you tense in his line

He wants you at training

And when you in training he wants you preparing yourself and being motivated because he doesn't want you slacking when time come

because when it time for his cadets to fall in place he doesn't want out of rack cadets

Just know when you face God when it time you better be ready

Just like war you gotta be ready when you in the war

You in a war when you fighting for souls

At time we feel left out because we look at people

And we look at ourselves we wish we was themselves

Instead of being happy for who we are and how God created us to be

Be careful when it comes down you wanting to be some body else

Because you don't know the Hell that person catch

Be yourself and know that you're a unique individual

And know that you're a blessed person because you're here

And know that people are way worst than the situation you're in

People are dyeing to be were you are so be thankful

people cared and watching you

You never know who has their eyes watching you

People you lease expected are

Count Your blessing and stop the complaining

Printed in the United States
By Bookmasters